BLESSED
JOHN PAUL II

VATICAN CITY – 1 MAY 2011

Index

"BLESSED JOHN PAUL II" Pocket edition
ISBN 978-88-89896-87-7

Publisher:
LOZZI ROMA s.a.s.
Via Filippo Nicolai, 91 - 00136 Roma
Tel. (+39) 06 35497051 - 06 97841668
Fax (+39) 06 35497074
E-mail: info@lozziroma.com
Printed by: CSC Grafica s.r.l. - Guidonia, Roma
Made in Italy

Photographs:
Archivio Lozzi Roma s.a.s.
Page 88, 89, Photo Scala, Florence
Page 12, 13, Archivio Farabola - Milano
For all of the other photos:

Servizio Fotografico
de L'Osservatore Romano
Città del Vaticano

We would like to thank the L'Osservatore Romano Photographic Service for its significant contribution.

Texts by Lozzi Roma s.a.s.

Gruppo Lozzi Editori: www.gruppolozzi.it

BEATUS IOANNES PAULUS II

An extraordinary story

Karol Józef Wojtyła was born on 18 May 1920 in Wadowice, a town about 50 km from Cracow in Poland. The first Polish pope in history, he was the first non-Italian pope to have been elected in 455 years (since Dutch Pope Adrian VI in the 16th century). Born to a family of humble origins and solid Christian faith, his father Karol Wojtyła Senior, who died in 1941, was a tailor and he served as a petty officer in the Austrian Army and later as a lieutenant in the Polish Army. His mother Emilia Kaczorowska died prematurely in 1929 before young Karol Wojtyła was even 9 years old.

The youngest of the couple's three children, his older sister Olga died before he was born. His brother Edmund was born on 27 August 1906 in Cracow and he worked as a physician at Powszechny Hospital in Bielsko before dying of scarlet fever in 1932.

Karol Józef Wojtyła was baptized on 20 June 1920 in the Wadowice parish church. He celebrated his First Communion at the age of 9 and he received the Sacrament of Confirmation at the age of 18. After graduating from "Marcin Wadowita" high school in Wadowice, he enrolled at the "Jagiellonian University" in Cracow where he received a degree in theology in 1946.

Ordained as a priest that same year by Cardinal Sapieha he then began his lively pastoral activity above all among

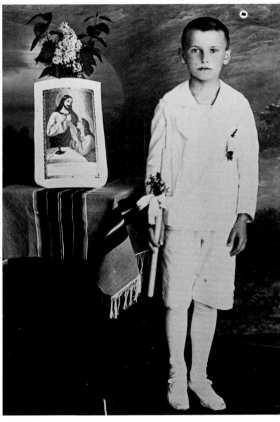

On the left: young Karol Wojtyła with his mother and father.

Above: Karol with his mother Emilia who died when he was 9 years old.
On the right: First Communion day..

with the labourers and young people. From the time he was an adolescent he had been attracted to recitation and theatre as a form of expression and communication. During the Nazi invasion of Poland (which began in September 1939) he took part in underground productions that were performed secretly at the homes of a group of friends. While attending university, he joined a theatre association named "Studio 38".

In 1943 he appeared for the last time on stage in an underground production of "Samuel Zborowski" by Juliusz Słowacki where he played the role of the protagonist. Karol Wojtyła was one of the promoters of "Rhapsodic Theatre" (founded in 1941) also known as "Theatre of the Word" or "Theatre of the Catacombs". When the occupying Nazi forces closed

the University in 1939, he was forced to find work as a labourer in a stone quarry in Zakrzówek near Cracow and then in 1942 at the Solvay chemical factory in order to earn a living and avoid deportation to Germany. This affected him deeply and it was an important life experience: "I was a labourer for four years and those four years were worth more to me than two college degrees" he said much later when speaking to Roman labourers in 1979.

Called to the priesthood, he began attending underground seminary training courses in 1942 in Cracow organised by the Archbishop of Cracow, Cardinal Adam Stefan Sapieha. He was later transferred to a secret seminary at the Archbishop's palace together with other students. He remained there until the end of the war and on 18 January 1945 the Red Army finally freed Cracow from Nazi control.

He was ordained a priest in 1946 and on November 2nd he celebrated his first Holy Mass in St. Leonard's Crypt at Wawel Cathedral. That same year he left Poland for Rome where he enrolled at the Pontifical University of Saint Thomas Aquinas, also known as the "Angelicum".

During his vacations he would preach to polish immigrants in France, Belgium and Holland.

In 1948 he left Rome and returned to Cracow where he received a doctorate in spiritual theology at "Jagiellonian University". Later he served as the vice parish priest, at the parish of Niegowić near Gmina Gdów and later in Cracow as the vice parish priest at St. Florian parish.

After that he served as chaplain at the University until 1951 when he returned to study philosophy and theology. In 1953 at the Catholic University of Lublin he presented his thesis entitled, "Evaluating the possibility of founding a Christian ethical system based on the ethical system of Max Scheler".

In those same years, Poland was moving towards becoming a Socialist Republic and it was falling increasingly more subject to the control of the Soviet Union.

In 1953 he was chosen as a University professor at the Jagiellonian University of Cracow where he taught Catholic social ethics at the Theology Faculty and later he taught at the Catholic University of Lublin.

As time progressed the relationship between the church and the Communist regime in Poland became increasingly difficult. The leader of the Polish church Cardinal Stefan Wyszynski was arrested and only released after three long years.

In 1958 at the age of 38, Karol Wojtyła was appointed as auxiliary bishop to the Archbishop of Cracow, Monsignor Eugeniusz Baziak, by Pope Pius XII, who died on 9 October of that same year. After the death of Archbishop Baziak he became the Vicar Capitular.

Later he participated in the works for the

Karol Wojtyła gives a boy an autograph.

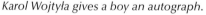

An intense close-up.

first and second session of Vatican Council II. Upon his return he was chosen as Metropolitan Archbishop of Cracow with a papal bull issued on 13 January 1964 and he worked at the Wawel Cathedral.

Later he took part in the third and fourth sessions of the Vatican II Council and provided an important contribution to the drafting of the Constitution *"Gaudium et spes"* (on the church in the contemporary world).

On 28 June 1967 he was ordained Cardinal by Pope Paul VI in the Sistine Chapel at the Vatican with the title of San Cesario in Palatio (the Church's youngest cardinal).

While he was a Cardinal, he took an active role in the life of the Church: he participated in the five assemblies of the Synod of Bishops before his pontificate and he made a number of trips and pilgrimages.

In 1978 he participated in the funeral for Paul VI, the pontifical inauguration ceremony and funeral of John Paul I (Albino Luciani), who died only one month after his pontificate began.

The conclave to elect a new pope began on 14 October and on 16 October at 5:15 PM Cardinal Karol Wojtyła was elected. He was the 264th successor of Peter and he had the third longest pontificate (27 years) in the history of the Church following Pius IX and St. Peter. He took the name John Paul II and his pontificate began solemnly on 22 October.

He guided the Church with authority, love and dedication giving a strong impulse and great significance to ecumenical dialogue - always working for the unity of all Christians.

As the Bishop of Rome he frequently visited the city parishes. However he will always be remembered for his many journeys to all corners of the globe. His desire was to be close to all peoples (and not just those of the Christian faith) to bring them moral and spiritual comfort and to fully complete his pastoral mission.

On 13 May 1981 in St. Peter's Square there was an assassination attempt against the Pope. The world was shocked as Turkish terrorist Ali Ağca fired two shots from a pistol and seriously injured the Pope. It was never clearly established who or what motivated the assassination attempt, but the event happened at a delicate moment of the world's history. There were days of apprehension as John Paul II fought against death and suffering with Christian courage and spirit.

In 2000, the church revealed that this terrible event was the third secret of Fatima. The secret revealed that the Bishop dressed in white (identified as the Holy Father) would die by assassination.

Later, John Paul II would attribute the deviation of the bullet to the Madonna:

"a maternal hand deviated the trajectory of the bullet".

The assassination attempt did sorely hinder the Pope's health in later years. He was unfortunately hospitalized a number of times for various reasons including a sprained arm, a fractured femur and later for other operations including colon cancer. The illness that physically troubled him the most was without a doubt Parkinson's Disease. Despite his health problems, he never forgot his pastoral mission around the globe.

He had an ability to truly motivate young people. He was always fond of them and had an extraordinary relationship with them up until the last instants of his life. In 1985 the Pope instituted World Youth Day which is celebrated every two years at a different site chosen by the Pope.

During his 27 year pontificate, "missionary" John Paul II travelled 1,247,000 kilometres and took 104 trips outside Italy to visit 131 countries in all of the continents. In 1989 he was still active and he participated in the delicate geopolitical transformation that was taking place in Eastern Europe. At the Vatican he met with Mikhail Gorbacev, who was the president of the Soviet Union at that time. The Pope's *Ostpolitik* policy did contribute to softening the impact of the fall of communism in Eastern Europe in the former Soviet Union, symbolically represented by the fall of the Berlin Wall.

In 1993 during a trip to Sicily, he expressed himself strongly against the mafia in front of tens of thousands of people: "God once said do not kill".

22 October 1979. John Paul II, a few days after his election, receives homage from Cardinal Ratzinger (future Pope Benedict XVI).

Pope Paul VI ordains Cardinal Karol Wojtyła, Rome 28 June 1967.

October 1979. John Paul II gives his first speech to the UN general assembly.

No human group, whether it is mafia or any other, may trample the most sacred law of God. In the name of the crucifixion and resurrection...convert. One day God's judgement will arrive".
John Paul II also criticized the "law of profit" which too frequently got the upper hand in the western world. He constantly urged the west and the capitalist world in general to limit consumption and develop more tangible genuine generosity towards the third and fourth world, by asking rich industrialised countries to cancel the debts of those states.
His heartfelt and imploring appeals for peace to all the governments of countries, both warring and non, were unceasing and this led to him being called the "Pope of peace". "Nothing is resolved by war, it is quite the contrary, everything is put in danger by war", was his message for Peace Day 1994. In 1995 Time Magazine proclaimed John Paul II as "Man of the Year".
During his long pontificate Pope John Paul II proclaimed: 482 saints and over 1300 beatifications greatly surpassing the number of canonizations

John Paul II meets the children during Jubilee 2000.

proclaimed by his predecessors. In the encyclical of 1993 *"Veritatis Splendor"* John Paul II explained the need to offer fundamental points of reference to the faithful: "The Church proposes the example of many saints who have given their testimony and defended the moral truth up to martyrdom, or who preferred death to even a single mortal sin".

He wrote a total of 14 Encyclical Letters, many of which repeated the principles of faith and the Church's position on certain arguments such as social justice, the defence of truth and Christian ethics.

Pope John Paul II celebrated two Jubilee years. In 1983 the extraordinary *Holy Year of the Redemption* was held on the 1950th anniversary of the death and resurrection of Christ. In his letter "With the Coming of the Third Millennium", John Paul II began to prepare for the Grand Jubilee of the year 2000. During that Jubilee year on March 12th he solemnly pronounced the *"Mea culpa"*

at St. Peter's for errors committed by the Church over the course of the centuries. The aspiration of the Church to be "one" always accompanied Pope John Paul II. With tangible gestures, meetings, travels and Encyclicals, he gave inspiration to the ecumenical path of the Church. In 1986 he made a great gesture of reconciliation by visiting the Rome Synagogue (the first Pope to ever do so) where he prayed together with the Jews referring to them "elder brothers".

On January 18, 2000 when the Holy Door at

St. Paul's Outside the Wall was opened, the Pope was together with Metropolitan Athanasius and the Archbishop of Canterbury George Carey. With delegations from 22 different Christian faiths at the event, it was the largest concentration of Christian churches after Vatican Council II.

During the diplomatic crisis which preceded the war against Iraq he defended

peace and the UN's role with a supreme and legitimate appeal by the peoples of the world. On 13 January 2003, just a few days before the bombing of Baghdad, John Paul II spoke to the diplomats received at the Vatican and affirmed strongly: "No to war! War is not always inevitable and it is always a loss for humanity".

His slowly declining health represented something heroic for the faithful and all humanity. It seemed like the more his body bent, the stronger his impulse and vitality to guide the Church grew.

John Paul II died on the evening of 2 April 2005. Over three million followers and many young people from all over the world for his funeral bore witness of the pain, admiration and gratitude felt for this loved and adored Pope – so much that the mass cheered together: "Santo Subito!" (Saint now!)

THE ELECTION

"I come from a faraway land.
If I make a mistake «corrict» me".

From his first public speech after being elected on 16 October 1978

The election of Pope John Paul II to the Papal throne took place after a painful unexpected event: the death of Pope John Paul I on 28 September 1978 after a pontificate lasting only 33 days.

In October of 1978 Cardinal Wojtyła returned to the Vatican to take part in his second conclave in less than two months. He entered the conclave as a cardinal elector and after 8 ballots he was elected Pope to his own and the world's amazement. He had tears streaming down his face when he turned and said the following words in Latin to the conclave: "With obedience in faith to Christ, my Lord, and with trust in the Mother of Christ and the Church, in spite of great difficulties, I accept."

On 16 October 1978 at the age of fifty-eight, he succeeded John Paul I. At the moment of his election he had initially intended to take the name Stanislaw I in honour of the patron saint of Poland. However, due to the fact that many cardinals pointed out that it was not a traditional Roman name, he chose John Paul II in commemoration of his predecessor.

At 6:40 pm Cardinal Pericle Felici stood before the anxious crowd gathered in St. Peter's Square and stated: "With great joy I announce... *Habemus Papam!*" A few minutes later the new Pope stood before the faithful on the balcony at the centre of the immense Basilica of St. Peter's in the Vatican. He gave a short speech defining himself as «the new Pope called from a distant country». He immediately overcame the diffidence of the Italian people who were looking at a foreign Pope for the first time in a very long time by saying "se mi sbaglio mi corrigerete!" which translates as something like "If I make a mistake, corrict me", which brought an applause from the crowd.

At the end of his speech he gave his first *Urbi et Orbi* benediction and it was broadcast worldwide. The next day the Pope celebrated mass with the College of Cardinals in the Sistine Chapel on October 22nd and solemnly began his pontificate as the 264th successor of Peter the Apostle.

John Paul II greets the cheering crowd in St. Peter's Square from the "Loggia delle Benedizioni" on the day he was elected.

WORLD TOURS

January 1979 - June 2003

"From the beginning of my Pontificate I have chosen to travel to the ends of the earth in order to show this missionary concern. My direct contact with peoples who do not know Christ has convinced me even more of the urgency of missionary activity".

IN MEXICO

"Urgent reforms and bold transformations are needed to break down the barriers of the human exploitation of humanity".

January 1979 - The first trip outside Italy

IN POLAND

"It is the return home. I am doing my best to keep my emotions under control".
2 June 1979

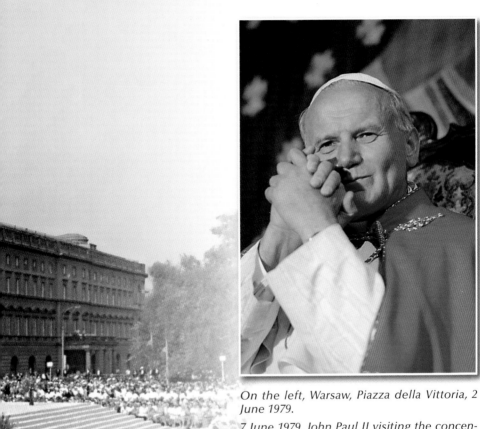

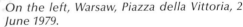

On the left, Warsaw, Piazza della Vittoria, 2 June 1979.

7 June 1979. John Paul II visiting the concentration camp Auschwitz-Birkenau.

"It is my nation, my homeland. I was born in this land, in this nation. I am its child and I carry the legacy of all its victories within me".
16 June 1983

"I am here in Poland to celebrate the Jubilee of the Redemption with all of my countrymen, especially those who have most painfully suffered the bitterness of disillusionment, humiliation, suffering – those who have been deprived of liberty, who have suffered prejudice and whose human dignity has been trodden upon".

16 June 1983

On the right, John Paul II praying in front of the Black Madonna icon of Czestochowa in 1983.

"The path of freedom is not without risk, however it has a very high price. The new climate of freedom does not resolve all of the problems of your lives by itself".
13-21 August 1991

On the left, John Paul II with a massive cheering crowd in Czestochowa in June 1979.

Below, photos taken during his pastoral visits in Poland. On the left in 1983 and on the right in 1991.

IN THE UNITED STATES

"The first of these systematic threats against human rights is linked in an overall sense with the distribution of material goods. This distribution is frequently unjust both within individual societies and on the planet as a whole".
October 1979

"I come in friendship as a friend of America and all Americans: Catholic, Orthodox, Protestant and Jewish faiths combined – people of every religion and all the men and women of good faith".
September 1987

IN AFRICA

"The church cannot offer technical solutions to the immense problems of the continents, but it is near all the African people to support them so that they can become the protagonists of their internal and international redemption".
Senegal, February 1992

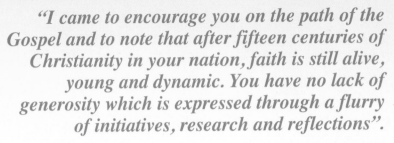

"I came to encourage you on the path of the Gospel and to note that after fifteen centuries of Christianity in your nation, faith is still alive, young and dynamic. You have no lack of generosity which is expressed through a flurry of initiatives, research and reflections".

May-June 1980

Upper left, the parade marches along Champs-Élysées in 1980. Below, in Lourdes 1979. Double page, Paris Champs de Mars in 1980.

IN THE UNITED KINGDOM

"I came here as a herald of peace, to proclaim a Gospel of peace and a message of reconciliation and love".
Cardiff, June 1982

IN INDIA

"He was never a Christian and never pretended to be, but I learned a lot from him. Christians should learn how to be Christians from him. I have learned a great deal from him and am not ashamed to admit it".

About Mahatma Ghandi, India 1986

IN SPAIN

"I want to ask young people to open their hearts to the Gospel and to be testimonies of Christ; and if necessary testimonies-martyrs at the threshold of the third millennium".
August 1989

Giovanni Paolo II percorre parte del cammino di Santiago de Compostela, Agosto 1989.

IN BRAZIL

"The Church in Brazil is the church of the poor. When thinking of the rich who are closed to God and men without mercy Christ cried: Watch out!".
July 1980

> *"A future of peace and secure liberty and justice may only exist if humanity and peoples become aware of the elements they share which unite them".*
>
> *June 1996*

John Paul II together with Cardinal Ratzinger in 1996.

IN AUSTRIA

"This Europe is a splendid product of the Christian message, but it is also full of defects [...], its unity is incomprehensible without the content of the Christian message".

September 1983

IN LITHUANIA

"From these lands forming a natural bridge between central-northern Europe and eastern Europe, I would like to send a special greeting to nearby Russia and in particular to the Christian communities".

Vilnius, September 1993

The Pope praying on the Hill of Crosses north of Šiauliai.

IN SLOVAKIA

"Do not confuse freedom with individualism! There is no genuine freedom without love for others. Christians live freedom as a service, convinced that the development of an authentic civilisation depends on this".
June 1995

IN PORTUGAL

"Accept, O Mother of Christ, this cry laden with the sufferings of all individual human beings, laden with the sufferings of whole societies".
May 1982

On the right, the Pope with Sister Mary Lucy of Jesus and of the Immaculate Heart, one of the three children who saw apparitions of Our Lady of Fatima. Below, praying to Our Lady of Fatima.

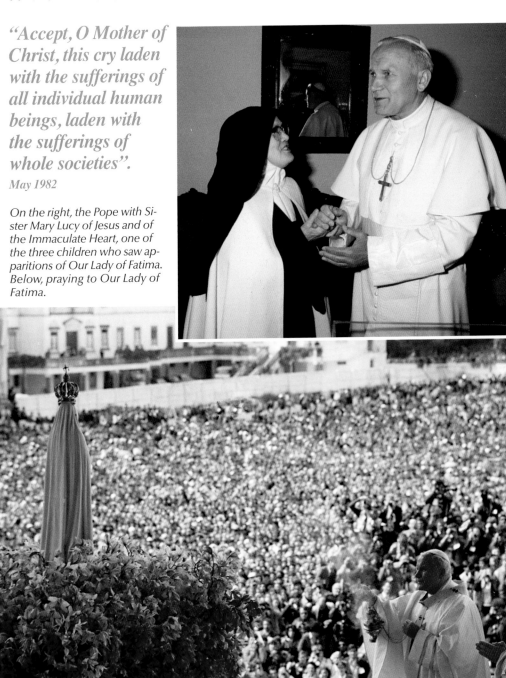

IN EGYPT

"Today as always, the Ten Words of the Law provide the only true basis for the lives of individuals, societies and nations".

February 2000

Mount Sinai - The Monastery of St. Catherine.

IN THE HOLY LAND

"In this area of the world there are grave and urgent issues of justice, of the rights of peoples and nations, which have to be resolved for the good of all concerned and as a condition for lasting peace".
March 2000

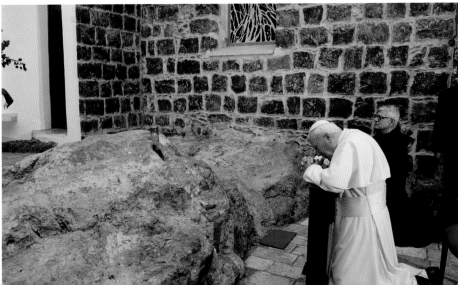

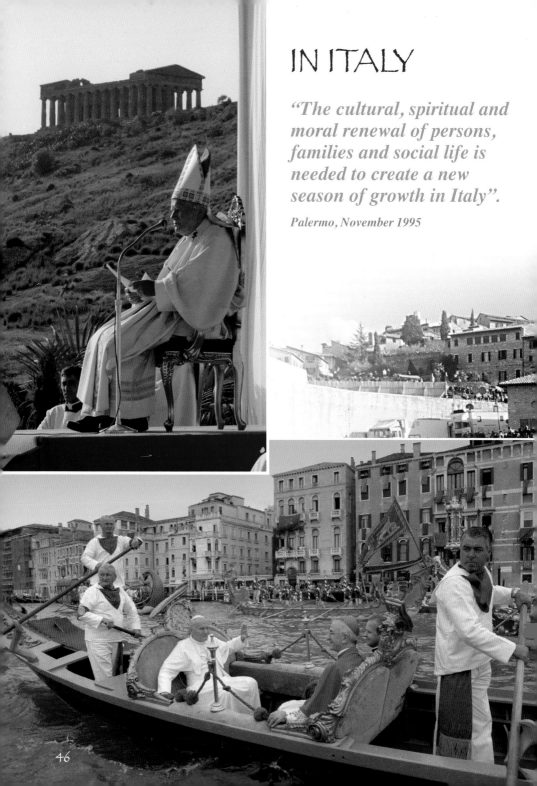

IN ITALY

"The cultural, spiritual and moral renewal of persons, families and social life is needed to create a new season of growth in Italy".

Palermo, November 1995

John Paul II during four stops on his Italian tour: Agrigento (on the left), Venice (below on the left), Maranello, the Ferrari headquarters (above), Assisi (below).

THE POPE FOR EVERYONE

"It is precisely on the path of the moral life that the way of salvation is open to all".
Encyclical "Veritatis Splendor" 1993

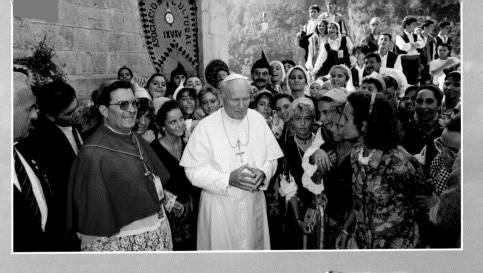

"Dear young people of the century now beginning, by saying 'yes' to Christ, you are saying 'yes' to all your noblest ideals. Have no fear to entrust yourselves to him. He will guide you, he will grant you the strength to follow him every day and in every situation".

"I have wished to encourage believers and all people of good will to promote respect for the dignity of every human being and to work for an international order built on respect for the rule of law and on solidarity with the less fortunate".

"Spend time in prayer, letting the Spirit speak to your hearts. To pray means to give some of your time to Christ, to entrust your lives, joining them to Christ, the Word made flesh".

John Paul II with Mother Teresa of Calcutta.

DEVOTION
TO THE MADONNA

*Below, the Pope celebrates mass in front of the Black Madonna of Czestochowa in Po-
land. On the right and page 58, the Holy Father in front of Our Lady of Fatima in Portugal.*

"Totus Tuus"

"It is a fundamental devotion in my life and I want to lead the Church in Marian prayer so that Mary can help us welcome the love of God into our hearts simply".

Lourdes, France August 1983

On the right, moments of prayer in the Grotto of Lourdes, France.

DIALOGUE WITH OTHER CHURCHES

"The future of peace in the world depends on strengthening dialogue and understanding between cultures and religions".

On the left, John Paul II and Teoctist, the Patriarch of Romania, 1999. On the right, in front of Al Aqsa Mosque with the Imam of Jerusalem in March 2000. Below. World Day of Prayer for Peace, Assisi. At the event there were 50 representatives from various Christian faiths (beyond Catholicism) and 60 representatives of other world religions.

"May the hearts of Christians and Muslims turn to one another with feelings of brotherhood and friendship".

CANONIZATIONS

"The Church proposes the example of numerous Saints who bore witness to and defended moral truth even to the point of enduring martyrdom, or who preferred death to a single mortal sin".

Encyclical "Veritatis Splendor" 1993

Below a crowd of followers in St. Peter's Square for the Canonization of Padre Pio on 16 June 2002.
Opposite page: on the left, the Canonization of Mary Faustyna Kowalska, 30 April 2000; on the right, the Canonization of Maximilian Maria Kolbe, 10 October 1982.

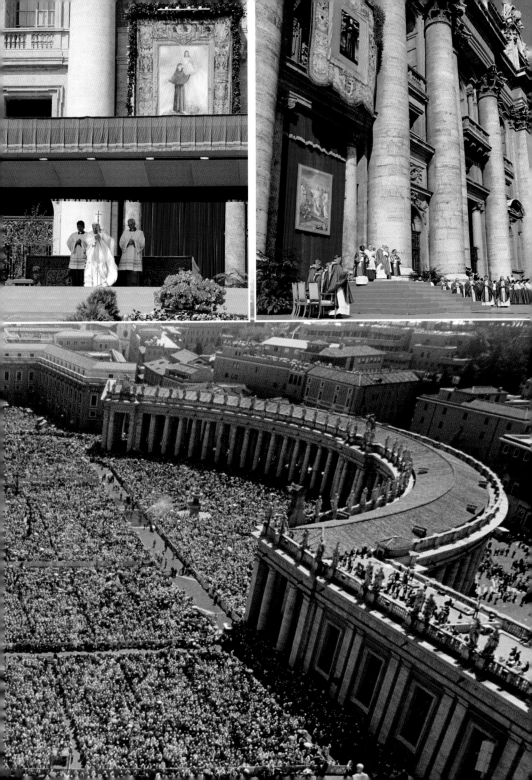

ASSASSINATION ATTEMPT

"One hand shot the bullet and another deflected the bullet".

Regarding the assassination attempt (13 May 1981), he attributed the deflection of the bullet to intervention by the Madonna.

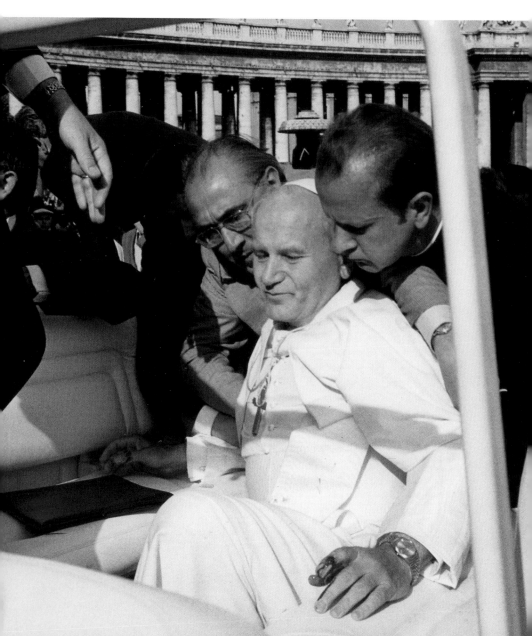

Two pictures after the attempt on the Pope's life 13 May 1981. Below, meeting in prison with Ali Ağca: the Turkish man who attempted to assassinate Pope John Paul II.

"Mother of God and men! We come to you in the Year of the Holy Redemption to venerate the incredible work that the Holy Trinity has completed through You, in the generation of Christ, Redeemer of the world and your son: in the Jubilee Year we thank God for You, first of the Redeemed; for you, preserved from original sin among all the children of Adam".
Rome, 1983

HOLY YEAR 1983~84
OF THE REDEMPTION

JUBILEE 2000

"Christ Son of the Virgin Mother, light and hope of those who seek you out even without knowing you and after knowing you search even harder; Christ, You are the Door! Through you in the power of the holy spirit, we want to enter the third millennium".

Rome, Christmas 1999

On the left, holy mass at the Sistine Chapel.
On the right, opening the Holy Door of St. Peter's Basilica to inaugurate the Jubilee Year.

NATURE

"Through all that is created the 'eyes of the mind' can come to know God".
Encyclical "Fides et Ratio" 1998

"How many Popes of St. Peter's know how to ski?" Answer: One".

"These mountains imbue the heart with a feeling of infinity and with the desire to raise the mind up to that which is sublime".

"The world can change!".

FAREWELL

"I have searched for you and now you have come to me and I thank you".

On his deathbed, 2 April 2005

BEATIFICATION
Vatican City, 1 May 2011

On 1 May 2011 Pope John Paul II was solemnly beatified in St. Peter's square by his successor Pope Benedict XVI.

When a person is beatified it means that the church formally recognizes that the defunct has ascended to heaven and is able to intercede on behalf of those who pray for intercession.

Sainthood is a much longer process and the process of canonization always follows the rite of beatification (one cannot become saint without having been beatified first). The announcement that millions of followers were anxiously expecting was delivered in a news brief by the Congregation for the Causes of Saints: "This 14 January 2011, Pope Benedict XVI during an audience granted to Cardinal Angelo Amato, Prefect of the congregation for the Causes of Saints, authorised the dicastery to promulgate the decree of the miracle attributed to the intercession of Venerable Servant of God, John Paul II (Karol Wojtyła).

This concludes the process which precedes the Rite of Beatification for which the date shall be decided by the Pope".

Later Vatican spokesman Father Lombardi announced, "The Beatification of Venerable Servant of God, John Paul II (Karol Wojtyła), shall take place at the Vatican on 1 May 2011 presided over by Supreme Pontiff Benedict XVI". Divine Mercy Sunday, which is linked to Polish nun Saint Faustina Kowalska, was chosen as the date. Both the saint and the holiday were very dear to Pope John Paul II and to the Polish people.

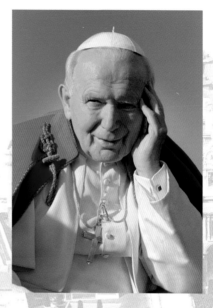

In contrast with church doctrine, the cause for the beatification was investigated very quickly (six years in all).

Normally at least five years must have passed since a death before the process can begin.

This happened for two reasons: papal approval was given in order to dispense with the usual five years and the Cause was transferred to a fast track process instead of working through the Congregation for the Causes of Saints.

For the Cause of beatification of Pope John Paul II, a great deal of work took place, an immense number of documents were examined and many testimonies were heard to analyse a pontificate that lasted 27 years and the entire life of a person who left a mark on the history of the nineteen hundreds. "It is well known – the Vatican announced – that by pontifical dispensation, his Cause began before the end of the five-year period which the current norms stipulate must pass following the death of a Servant of God.

This provision was solicited by the great fame of sanctity which Pope John Paul II

Suor Marie Simon-Pierre, guarita dal morbo di Parkinson per intercessione di Giovanni Paolo II.

enjoyed during his life, in his death and after his death. In all other ways, the normal canonical dispositions concerning causes of beatification and canonisation were observed in full".

Accelerating the cause of beatification, according to former Vatican Press spokesman Navarro Valls "simply confirms the sanctity with which the Pontiff lived. The figure of John Paul II goes beyond the confines of Catholicism. That is why I am not surprised to hear pleasure expressed in non-Catholic circles as well".

This was not the only exception in history. An important precedent in recent times was Mother Teresa of Calcutta. At that time John Paul II made a similar decision: the founder of the "Missionaries of Charity" died in 1997 and she was beatified on 19 October 2003.

In that case the Pope waited two years before starting the process, but there were no obstacles to the Cause. The process took a total of 6 years for Mother Theresa.

Between June 2005 and April 2007 the diocesan investigation and rogatory very accurately inspected the life, virtue, famed sanctity and miracles of Pope John Paul II. In June 2009 after examining the "Positio", nine theologians of the Dicastery confirmed the heroic nature of the virtues. Therefore on 19 December 2009, Pope Benedict XVI authorised the promulgation of the decree.

With a view to the beatification of the Venerable Servant of God John Paul II, the postulator of the cause invited the Congregation of the Causes of Saints to investigate Sister Marie Simon-Pierre's seemingly miraculous recovery from Parkinson's disease.

Sister Marie of the Institut des Petites Soeurs des Maternités Catholiques was diagnosed with the disease in 2001 by her physician and other specialists. She was treated for the illness, and though her symptoms became less severe, they continued.

Upon hearing of the death of Pope John Paul II, sister Marie and the other sisters at her institution began to pray to him (who had suffered the same illness) to be healed. On 2 June 2005, tired and oppressed by

The crowd in St. Peter's Square cheering - Saint now!

her pain, Sister Marie requested to be exonerated from her duties. However her Mother Superior asked her to seek comfort in prayer and to trust in the intercession of John Paul II.

Awaking after a peaceful night, Sister Marie felt that something extraordinary had happened: the pain was gone and she no longer felt the stiffness in her limbs that had been making her suffer just a few hours earlier.

It was 3 June 2005: Sacred Heart holy day. Sister Marie immediately went to her doctor who was amazed to confirm she had been healed.

On 21 October 2010, the canonical inquest and the detailed medical and legal analysis were examined by a medical consultant of the dicastery of the Causes of Saints.

On December 14, 2010 after reviewing the medical assessments, the theological consulters proceeded with theological evaluation of the case and unanimously recognized its uniqueness, its antecedent and the choral invocation addressed to

Pages 88 and 89, inside St. Peter's Basilica where the tomb of Blessed John Paul II is placed near the Confessional altar.

the Servant of God John Paul II, whose intercession was effective for miraculous healing."

Finally, on 11 January 2011, the Ordinary Session of the Cardinals and Bishops of the Congregation for the Causes of Saints was held. A unanimous affirmative ruling decided that Sister Marie Simon-Pierre's recovery was miraculous and scientifically inexplicable, and that it was a result of intercession by Pope John Paul II, faithfully invoked by the healed Sister Marie, as well as by many other faithful".

THE TOMB

The venerated tomb of Blessed John Paul II is located in one of the altars in the right nave of St. Peter's Basilica. Various projects were designed by basilica archpriest Cardinal Angelo Comastri, but Pope Ratzinger decided that it should be moved from the Vatican Grottoes, where it has been located since the funeral, to the Chapel of St. Sebastian on the right of the central nave between the Chapel that holds Michelangelo's Pietà and the Chapel of the Holy Sacrament.

BLESSED JOHN PAUL II

John Paul II in 1989 while travelling to Spain.

EVENTS AND FACTS ABOUT HIS PONTIFICATE

Trips inside Italy

Number of Trips	146
Number of cities visited (minus the repetitions)	259
Number of trips outside Rome and Castelgandolfo	307
Number of scheduled speeches	906
Total duration	278 days 23h 35m¹
Total number of kilometres travelled	84,998

International trips

International trips of John Paul II	104
Number of trips to countries outside Italy	205
Number of nations visited (without repetitions)	129
Number of visits to various locations	715
Number of locations visited	617
Public speeches during his international travels	2,382
Overall duration of his international travels	543 days
Total kilometres travelled internationally	1,162.615
Days of John Paul II's Pontificate	9,666
Distance in kilometres of the earth's circumference	40,000
Average distance between the earth and the moon in kilometres	384,440
Relationship with the distance between the Earth and the Moon	3,02

The Pontifical Statistics

- 3rd longest pontificate in history.
- 3 Exorcisms
- 6 Hospitalisations.
- 9 Consistories.
- 11 Apostolic Constitutions.
- 14 Encyclicals.
- 14 Apostolic Exhortations.
- 28 Motu proprio documents.
- 38 Official visits with Heads of State.
- 52 Canonization Ceremonies.
- 104 Trips.
- 129 Nations visited.
- 145 Beatification Ceremonies.
- 226 Prime Ministers received for audience.
- 232 Cardinals nominated (in 9 Consistories).
- 274 Anointing of the Sick sacraments.
- 300 Confessions.
- 301 Parish visits.
- 482 Saints proclaimed.
- 697 Cities visited.
- 703 Interviews with Heads of State.
- 738 Meetings with Heads of State.
- 740 Visits to the Diocese in Rome.
- 1,164 General Audiences.
- 1,339 Beatifications proclaimed.
- 1,378 Baptisms.
- 1,595 Confirmations.
- 2,125 Priests Ordained.
- 2,412 Public speeches.
- 1,163.865 Kilometres travelled by plane – three times the distance between the Earth and the Moon.

Beatifications

147 celebrations;
86 at the Vatican;
61 outside the Vatican;
1,341 Beatifications proclaimed

Canonizations

52 celebrations;
38 at the Vatican;
14 outside the Vatican;
482 Saints proclaimed

Works and documents published by John Paul II

Papal Bulls
Aperite Portas Redemptori, 6 January 1983.
Incarnationis mysterium, 29 November 1998.

Apostolic Constitutions
Sapientia Christiana (Christian Wisdom), 15 April 1979.
Scripturarum Thesaurus (The Treasure of the Scriptures), 25 April 1979.
Magnum Matrimonii Sacramentum (The Great Sacrament of Matrimony), 7 October 1982.
Sacrae Disciplinae Leges (The Laws of Canonical Discipline), 25 January 1983.
Divinus Perfectionis Magister (The Divine Teacher and Model of Perfection), 25 January 1986.
Spirituali militum curae (On the Spiritual Care of the Military), 21 April 1986.
Pastor Bonus (The Good Shepherd), 28 June 1988.
Ex Corde Ecclesiae (Born From the Heart of the Church), 15 August 1990.
Fidei Depositum (The Deposit of Faith), 11 October 1992.
Universi Dominici Gregis (The Shepherd of the Lord's Whole Flock),
22 February 1996
Ecclesia in Urbe, (The Church in the City), 1 January 1998.

Encyclicals
Redemptor Hominis (The Redeemer of Man), 4 March 1979.
Dives in Misericordia (Rich in Mercy), 30 November 1980.
Laborem Exercens (On Human Work), 14 September 1981.
Slavorum Apostoli (The Apostles of the Slavs), 2 June 1985.
Dominum et Vivificantem (On the Holy Spirit
in the Life of the Church and the World), 18 May 1986.
Redemptoris Mater (The Mother of the Redeemer), 25 March 1987.
Sollicitudo Rei Socialis
(The Social Concern of the Church), 30 December 1987
Redemptoris Missio (The Mission of Christ the Redeemer),
7 December 1990.
Centesimus Annus (On the Hundredth Anniversary
of Rerum Novarum), 1 May 1991.
Veritatis Splendor (The Splendour of Truth), 6 August 1993.
Evangelium Vitae (The Gospel of Life), 25 March 1995.
Ut Unum Sint (On Commitment to Ecumenism), 25 May 1995.
Fides et Ratio (Faith and Reason), 14 September 1998.
Ecclesia de Eucharistia (On the Eucharist in its
Relationship to the Church), 17 April

Apostolic Exhortations
Catechesi Tradendae (16 October 1979).
Familiaris Consortio (22 November 1981).
Redemptionis Donum (25 March 1984).
Reconciliatio et paenitentia (2 December 1984).
Christifideles laici (30 December 1988).
Redemptoris Custos (15 August 1989).
Pastores dabo vobis (25 March 1992).
Ecclesia in Africa (14 September 1995).
Vita consecrata (25 March 1996).
A New Hope for Lebanon (10 May 1997).
Ecclesia in America (22 January 1999).
Ecclesia in Asia (6 November 1999).
Ecclesia in Oceania (22 November 2001).
Ecclesia in Europa (28 June 2003).
Pastores gregis (16 October 2003).

Motu proprio
Familia a Deo Instituta (9 May 1981).
Tredecim Anni (6 August 1982).
Recognito Iuris Canonici Codice (2 January 1984).
Dolentium Hominum (11 February 1985).
Quo Civium Iura (21 November 1987).
Sollicita Cura (26 December 1987)
Decessores Nostri (18 June 1988).
Iusti Iudicis (28 June 1988).
Ecclesia Dei (2 July 1988).
Institution of the Labour Office of the Holy See (ULSA) (1 January 1989).
Europae Orientalis (15 January 1993).
Inde a Pontificatus (25 March 1993).
Socialium Scientiarum (1 January 1994).
Vitae Mysterium (11 February 1994).
Definitive Statute establishing the Labour Office of the Holy See (30 September 1994).
Stella Maris (31 January 1997).
Ad Tuendam Fidem (18 May 1998).
Apostolos Suos (21 May 1998).
Inter Munera Academiarum (28 January 1999).
Spes Aedificandi (1 October 1999).
Proclaiming Saint Thomas More Patron of Statesmen and Politicians (31 October 2000).
The new Fundamental Law of the State of the Vatican City (26 November 2000).
Sacramentorum sanctitatis (10 January 2002).
Misericordia Dei (2 May 2002).
Entrusting the management of the Pontifical Institute "Notre Dame of Jerusalem Centre" to the Legion of Christ (26 November 2004).

Other
Reform of the Code of Canon Law (25 January 1983).
Code of Canons of the Eastern Churches (18 October 1990).

Personal Writings

Italian Books
Strade d'amore.
Pensieri sparsi. Coraggiosi nella verità generosi nell'amore.
Pregherò per voi.
Non uccidere in nome di Dio.
Aprite i vostri cuori.
Sia pace!.
La bottega dell'orefice (1960).
Pietra di luce (1979).
Parole sull'uomo (1989).
Varcare la soglia della speranza (1994).
Non temiamo la verità (1995).
Maria, Maria stella del mattino. Chi prega ha in mano il timone della propria vita (1997).
Un invito alla gioia (1999).
Padre... (1999).
Fondare la civiltà dell'amore. Preghiere e meditazioni (2001).
Trittico romano. Meditazioni (2003).
Alzatevi, andiamo! (2004).
Memoria e Identità: Conversazioni a cavallo dei millenni (2005).

Musical Works
Rosary in French, English, Italian, Latin and Spanish; Sony Music (1994).
Rosary in Portuguese; Sony Music (1995).
Abbà Pater compact disc in 5 different languages; Sony Music (1999).
Mai più la guerra; EMI Music (2003).

Prayer for merciful intercession
of the Blessed John Paul II

O Holy Trinity,
we thank you for having graced the church with Pope John Paul II
and for allowing the tenderness of your fatherly care,
the glory of the cross of Christ and the splendour of the Holy Spirit
to shine through him.
Trusting fully in your infinite mercy and in the maternal intercession of Mary,
he has given us a living image of Jesus the Good Shepherd,
and has shown us that holiness is the necessary measure of ordinary Christian life
and is the way of achieving eternal communion with you.
Grant us, by his intercession, and according to your will,
the graces we implore,
hoping that he will soon be numbered among your saints.
Amen.

With ecclesiastic approval, Card. Camillo Ruini.

Joannes Paulus PP. II